November

K. C. KELLEY • BOB OSTROM

The Child's World

Published by The Child's World®
1980 Lookout Drive • Mankato, MN 56003-1705
800-599-READ • www.childsworld.com

Acknowledgments
The Child's World®: Mary Berendes, Publishing Director
The Design Lab: Design
Jody Jensen Shaffer: Editing and Fact-Checking

Photo credits
©andylid/iStock.com: 23 (bottom); Blulz60/iStock.com:
13 (bottom); carrie-nelson/Shutterstock.com: 23 (middle);
CEFutcher/iStock.com: 12 (top); Chris from Paris/Shutterstock.
com: 12 (bottom); Danredrup/Dreamstime.com : 22 (top); Denis
Rozhnovsky/Shutterstock.com: 20 (top); Georgios Kollidas/
Shutterstock.com: 19 (top); Hurst Photo/Shutterstock.com:
11 (bottom); Igorkali/Dreamstime.com: 6 (right); Ingemar
Magnusson/Dreamstime.com: 6 (left); Jaimie Duplass/Shutterstock.
com: 11(top); Joe Robbins: 23 (top); Markwaters/Dreamstime.
com: 22 (bottom); Michele Loftus/Dreamstime.com : 19
(bottom); Monkey Business Images/Dreamstime.com: cover, 1, 5;
mountainpix/Shutterstock.com: 18; NinaM/Shutterstock.com: 13
(top); risteski goce/Shutterstock.com: 10; Vacclav/Shutterstock.
com: 20 (bottom)

ISBN 9781626873711
LCCN 2014930710

Printed in the United States of America
Mankato, MN
July, 2014
PA02214

ABOUT THE AUTHOR

K.C. Kelley has written dozens of books for young readers on
everything from sports to nature to history. He was born in
January, loves April because that's when baseball begins, and
loves to take vacations in August!

ABOUT THE ILLUSTRATOR

Bob Ostrom has been illustrating books for twenty years.
A graduate of the New England School of Art & Design at
Suffolk University, Bob has worked for such companies as
Disney, Nickelodeon, and Cartoon Network. He lives in North
Carolina with his wife and three children.

Contents

WELCOME TO NOVEMBER!

Did it just get darker outside? There's a reason for that. It's November! For the past several years, Daylight Savings Time has ended each year in November. Nights are longer and days are shorter. But the beginning of November also means that Thanksgiving is nearly here. That's great news for everyone…except turkeys!

November

FACT BOX

Order: Eleventh

Days: 30

WHY DAYLIGHT SAVINGS?

We move the clocks back one hour in the fall and one hour ahead in the spring. This creates longer summer evenings…but makes winter nights short. In most places, that works fine, since it's too cold to be out at night in winter! Daylight Savings Time has been official in the United States since 1966.

HOW DID NOVEMBER GET ITS NAME?

In the original Roman calendar, the ninth month took its name from the Latin for the number nine: *novem*. Even after the calendar changed to 12 months, November kept its original name.

Birthstone

Each month has a stone linked to it. People who have birthdays in that month call it their birthstone. November has two birthstones (left to right): topaz and citrine (sih-TREEN).

NOVEMBER AROUND THE WORLD

Here is the name of this month
in other languages.

Chinese	Shí yī yuè
Dutch	November
English	November
French	Novembre
German	der November
Italian	Novembre
Japanese	Juuichigatsu
Spanish	Noviembre
Swahili	Novemba

TIME TO VOTE

Most places in the United States hold Election Day on the second Tuesday in November. Every four years, Election Day includes voting for president.

BIG NOVEMBER HOLIDAYS

Thanksgiving, Final Thursday

On the final Thursday of November, Americans stop to give thanks. This holiday is based on an early Pilgrim celebration. Giving thanks for a good harvest is an even older tradition. America's Thanksgiving became official in 1863. President Abraham Lincoln made it a national holiday during the Civil War. Today, Thanksgiving Day is celebrated with big family dinners, football games, and church services.

Veterans' Day, November 11

A veteran is a person who has served in a nation's military forces. November 11 has been celebrated in honor of America's veterans since 1919. Why November 11? On that date in 1918, World War I came to an end. The holiday was called Armistice Day at first. An armistice means an agreement to end a war. In 1954, the holiday became Veterans' Day to include vets from all of America's wars.

GIVING BACK, TOO

Many communities have events to help the less fortunate on Thanksgiving. School and church groups serve free Thanksgiving dinners. People can get free clothing at other places. In Santa Barbara, California, each year, an international medical charity welcomes hundreds of volunteers. They make "care packages" for victims of disasters. Then the volunteers head home for turkey!

FUN NOVEMBER DAYS

November has more ways to celebrate than just eating turkey! Here are some of the unusual holidays you can enjoy in November:

November 3

National Sandwich Day

November 6

Saxophone Day

November 13

World Kindness Day

November 15

America Recycles Day

WE RECYCLE

November 17

National
Take a Hike
Day

November 21

World
Hello Day

November 22

National Cashew Day

November 29

Square Dance Day

NOVEMBER WEEKS AND MONTHS

Holidays don't just mean days…you can celebrate for a week, too! You can also have fun all month long. Find out more about these ways to enjoy November!

NOVEMBER WEEKS

Geography Awareness Week: Geography is the study of our world and the places on it. Ask your teacher to show you a few things about geography. Can you find your state on a map? What about your city?

National Young Readers' Week: Make sure and read this book again the second week in November. You'll join millions of kids celebrating the fun and surprise of reading.

National Game and Puzzle Week: This week is about puzzles, brainteasers, pencil games, and more. Turn off the screens and grab your dice and play!

NOVEMBER MONTHS

Native American Heritage Month: The first people to live in North America had a rich history and culture. They still do! Events in this month celebrate Native Americans. Listen to music, check out art, and hear the stories of these diverse groups.

National Novel Writing Month: Every year, more than 100,000 people sign up to write a novel—in a month! It's called "NaNoWriMo" for short. Writers add their daily total of words and try to reach 50,000 in 30 days. Why don't you give it a try?

National Model Railroad Month: Do you like model trains? This is the month to celebrate them! Fans of model railroads get really into their hobbies. Find a model railroad club in your area this month. Ask if you can come and see their trains in action. All aboard!

NOVEMBER AROUND THE WORLD

Countries around the world celebrate in November. Find these countries on the map. Then read about how people there have fun in November!

November 19

Discovery Day, Puerto Rico
On this day in 1493, Christopher Columbus arrived in Puerto Rico. Its citizens remember the day each year with parties and parades.

DAY OF THE DEAD

People in Mexico and many Latin American countries call November 1–2 as *Dia de los Muertos,* or "the Day of the Dead." They wear colorful costumes and make shrines to their relatives. Skull candles are lit and parades are common.

November 30

St. Andrew's Day, Scotland
This is a big holiday in Scotland. Andrew is the patron saint of this part of the United Kingdom.

November 11

King's Birthday, Bhutan
Jigme Singye Wangchuck was king of this tiny Asian country from 1972–2008.

November 13

World Kindness Day
Since 1997, many countries have used this day to help people understand the importance of kindness to each other.

NOVEMBER IN HISTORY

November 1, 1993

Twelve countries created the **European Union**. They work together to unify Europe. Today, there are 28 members of the E.U.

November 4, 1922

Howard Carter discovered King Tut's tomb in Egypt.

GETTYSBURG ADDRESS

On November 19, 1863, President Abraham Lincoln gave one of the most famous speeches ever. He was in Gettysburg, Pennsylvania, to dedicate a cemetery. His talk was only two minutes long, but his words echo today: "Four score and seven years ago...." Look it up and read it together!

November 6, 1429

Henry VI became king of England. He was only eight years old!

November 7, 1917

The Russian Revolution created what became the Communist Soviet Union.

November 9, 1989

The Berlin Wall came down. The wall had divided Berlin, Germany, for nearly 30 years into East and West parts.

November 17, 1800

The U.S. Congress met in Washington D.C. for the first time. Earlier U.S. capitals had been in Philadelphia and New York City.

A TIME FOR PEACE

THE BERLIN WALL
AUG 13, 1961 NOV 9, 1989
FORGET NOT THE TYRANNY OF THIS WALL HORRID PLACE. NOR THE LOVE OF FREEDOM THAT MADE IT FALL — LAID WASTE.

November 18, 1993

South Africa approved a new constitution. For the first time in more than 300 years, black and white people were equal in that country.

November 21, 1783

Two men in France became the first people to ride in a hot-air balloon.

November 22, 1963

President John F. Kennedy was shot and killed in Dallas, Texas.

NEW STATES!

Six states first joined the United States in November. Do you live in any of these? If you do, then make sure and say, "Happy Birthday!" to your state.

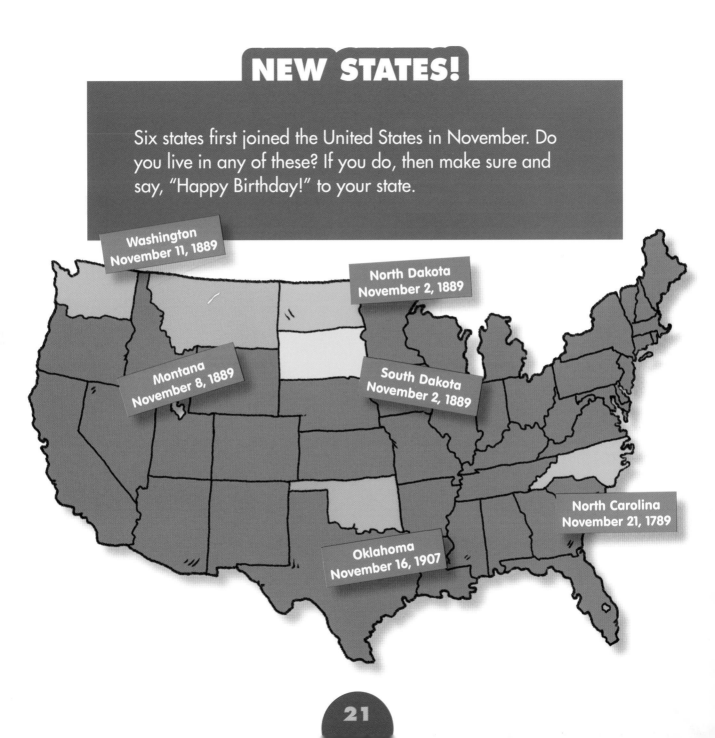

Washington
November 11, 1889

North Dakota
November 2, 1889

Montana
November 8, 1889

South Dakota
November 2, 1889

North Carolina
November 21, 1789

Oklahoma
November 16, 1907

FAMOUS NOVEMBER BIRTHDAYS

November 7

Madame Marie Curie
A famous scientist, she was the first woman to win a Nobel Prize.

November 14

Prince Charles
This son of England's Queen Elizabeth II is first in line to take over her job someday!

November 14

Condoleezza Rice
She was the Secretary of State from 2005–2009 and now helps run Stanford University.

November 18

David Ortiz

The slugger they call "Big Papi" has helped the Boston Red Sox win three World Series.

November 26

Charles Schulz

The famous cartoonist created the comic strip "Peanuts."

November 27

Bill Nye

Known as "The Science Guy," he appears on TV teaching science to kids.

November 30

Sir Winston Churchill

A longtime leader in Great Britain, he was Prime Minister during World War II.

GLOSSARY

Armistice (AR-miss-tiss) A temporary agreement to stop fighting a war.

diverse (dy-VERSS) Varied or assorted.

European Union (yur-uh-PEE-yun YOON-yun) A group of European countries that work together on many different things.

Pilgrim (PIL-grim) The Pilgrims were a group of people who left England for America around 1620.

veteran (VET-ur-un) Someone who has served in the military, especially during a war.

INDEX